CONTENTS

CONTENTS

What's happening to me?

THE BODYCLOCK

You're changing. The jeans that you bought a couple of months ago are now too small. You've outgrown your trainers. You seem to be growing more every day. Your voice is sounding different and you're starting to grow hair where you've never had hair before. What's happening?
It's called puberty.

Puberty

Puberty is the time in your life when you change from being a child to being an adult. It doesn't happen overnight – it takes a few years. Everyone goes through puberty. It's just part of growing up.

During puberty, you will experience many changes, both to the way your body looks and to the way you feel. This book will help you understand the changes you are going through.

Your bodyclock

Each of us has our own bodyclock, from the time we are born. Your bodyclock tells your body how fast to grow and when to start changing. Puberty only happens when your body is ready to grow. You can't stop it or hurry it up. Puberty starts to happen between the ages of about eight and seventeen years old. But we don't all change at exactly the same age.

Debbie: 'My sister's older than me so I know what to expect. It's good to have someone to talk to about things that are worrying me.'

Jamie: 'I'm not sure I want to change. I like my life the way it is now.'

Hormones

Puberty happens because of hormones. Hormones are chemicals made by your body. At puberty, more hormones are made. They start pumping round your body in your blood. They tell parts of your body to grow and change and start making sex hormones. Sex hormones change your body shape and get it ready so you can have babies if you want to when you are older.

How do you know when puberty has started?

You see signs that your body is changing. This book will tell you the signs to look for and help you understand the changes.

What if it doesn't start?

It will. Everyone goes through puberty. Don't worry if some of your friends start changing before you do. Remember, everyone has their own bodyclock. Your bodyclock is right and normal for you.

Feelings

As you grow up, your body changes and your feelings change too. You may find your moods going up and down. One day you may feel really happy. The next day you may feel really sad. You may want to spend more time alone, or with your friends rather than your family. You start to feel more like an adult and it's hard if people still treat you like a child.

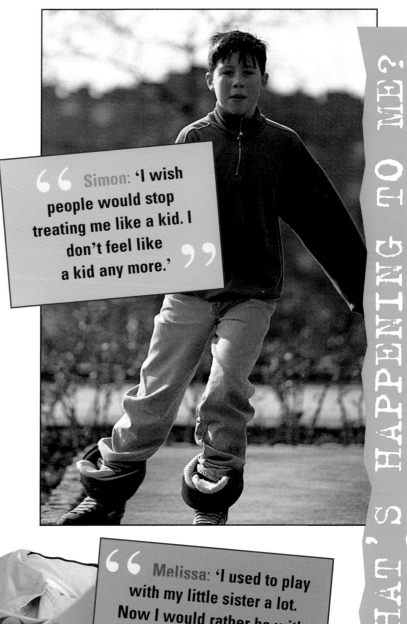

Simon: 'I wish people would stop treating me like a kid. I don't feel like a kid any more.'

Melissa: 'I used to play with my little sister a lot. Now I would rather be with my friends, or on my own listening to my favourite music.'

GROWING UP

Growth spurt

The first change that happens is that you start to grow a lot. This happens to girls when they are about eight to eleven years old, and to boys when they are about ten to thirteen years old. You can grow as much as 5–12 cm in a year.

For a while, girls may be taller than boys of the same age. This is because girls start growing fast before boys. Boys do catch up, and continue to grow when the girls have stopped. Girls reach their full height when they are about seventeen years old. Boys go on growing until they are about nineteen years old.

" Jake: 'I used to be about the same height as everyone else in my class. Now most of my friends are taller than me.' "

Try not to worry if some of your friends are growing taller or faster than you are. You may start your growth spurt later than them. Your final height depends on how tall your parents and grandparents are.

Tips for healthy growth

You can help your body while it is growing and changing by eating a healthy diet and getting plenty of exercise and sleep. Foods such as chicken, fish, eggs, cheese and nuts contain protein which helps your body grow.

Samantha: '**I'm really tall for my age. My mum and dad are both really tall. I'm worried about being taller than boys I meet.**'

What else is new?

CHANGING SHAPE

As you grow, your body starts changing shape too. Your arms and legs grow longer, and your hands and feet get bigger. Your head gets bigger, and even the shape of your face changes. Your nose, chin and forehead begin to grow larger and change shape.

Getting stronger

You start putting on weight fast. Much of the weight you put on turns to muscle, so your body gets stronger as it gets bigger. Inside your body, your main organs are growing too. Your lungs grow bigger and your heart almost doubles in weight. Even your blood changes as the number of red blood cells increases.

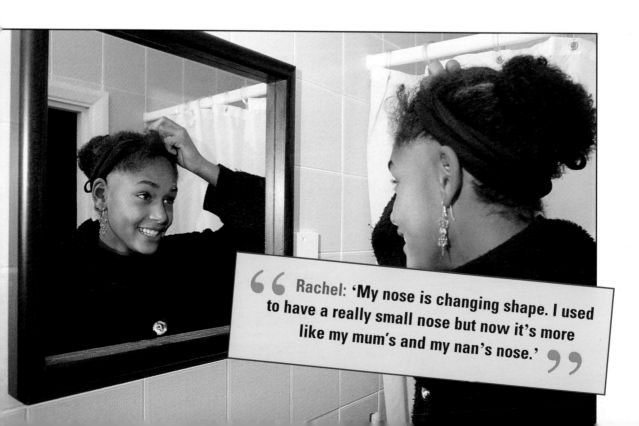

Rachel: 'My nose is changing shape. I used to have a really small nose but now it's more like my mum's and my nan's nose.'

Sounding different

Both boys' and girls' voices start to change and get deeper. This is because the voice box, called the larynx, is growing bigger. Boys' voices 'break' as they start to change. This means that their voices can sometimes sound high and squeaky, then suddenly go deeper. Eventually, their voices stay at the deeper tone.

▼ Boy's voices can sound funny when they start to break.

Peter: 'It was really strange when my voice started to break. It can happen in the middle of a sentence.'

Boys' changes

The hormones now pumping round your body make your sex parts grow. The sex parts between your legs are called your genitals.

At puberty, a boy's testicles start to grow. They hang in a soft bag of skin called the scrotum. The left testicle usually hangs lower than the right one. At puberty, the scrotum gets bigger and the skin becomes darker and wrinkled. The penis begins to grow and get longer and thicker.

Am I normal?

It's normal to worry that your sex parts aren't growing right or are different from everyone else's. Sex parts vary a lot in size, shape and colour. They are as different as people's noses and mouths are.

▼ *This diagram shows how your body changes during puberty.*

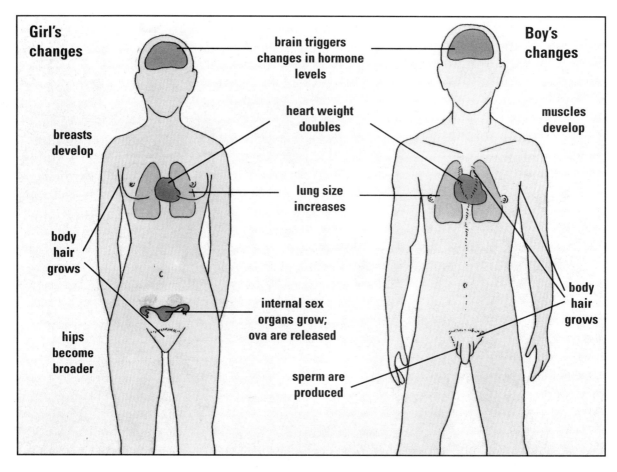

Girl's changes

Boy's changes

brain triggers changes in hormone levels

heart weight doubles

muscles develop

breasts develop

lung size increases

body hair grows

body hair grows

internal sex organs grow; ova are released

hips become broader

sperm are produced

Girls' changes

Girls will notice changes in their sex parts too. Between a girl's legs is her vagina. The vagina is an opening in the body that can stretch when a girl has sex and when a baby is being born. Around it are two pairs of fleshy lips called the labia. Just under the labia, where they meet at the front, is the clitoris, which is only the size of a pea. Girls can masturbate by rubbing or stroking their clitoris.

66 Jackie: 'I read about the clitoris in one of my magazines. I didn't know exactly where it was, so I took a look between my legs using a mirror.' 99

66 Dan: 'It can get embarrassing in the showers after rugby when everyone starts comparing how big they are. But I've heard people say size doesn't matter.' 99

New outlines

The outline of your body is changing shape too. Boys' chests and shoulders get broader, and their muscles start to grow. Girls get broader hips (ready for when they have babies) and their breasts start to grow.

During puberty, boys can sometimes feel a bit sore around their nipples and feel that their breasts are growing. This happens because of the sex hormones working overtime in your body. It stops as soon as your hormones settle down.

Jason: 'My brother and his mates work out at a gym. They call me skinny and names like that. I feel that I'll never catch up.'

A girl's nipples get darker and stand out more, and the breasts become fuller and rounder. Breasts vary a lot in size and shape. One may be slightly bigger than the other. They may feel tender to touch. Inside a girl's breasts are special glands that make milk if she has a baby.

It is worth getting measured properly for a bra to make sure you are wearing the correct size.

18

> Joanna: 'I was one of the first in my class to start wearing a bra. I don't wear it all the time, but I always wear it when we're doing sports.'

Girls may decide to start wearing a bra. Bras can help breasts stay in shape and make a girl more comfortable when playing sport.

BODY HAIR

The hormones working in your body make hair start to grow on your face, arms, legs and around your sex parts.

Body hair can start growing at any time between the ages of about nine and eighteen. Dark hair shows up more on the body than fair hair.

The hair around your sex parts is called your pubic hair. It is quite thin and soft at first but gets thicker and stronger.

Pubic hair and the hair under your arms can be a different colour from the hair on your head.

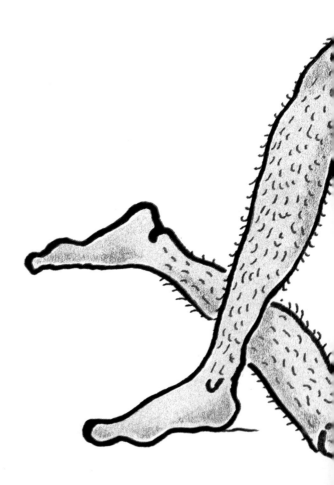

Boys usually have more body and face hair than girls. Hair starts growing above a boy's top lip, then on the cheeks and chin. Some hair may grow on the shoulders, the back of the hands and the toes and feet.

Some boys also grow hair on their chests and lower on the body. How much hair boys grow depends on how much the other men in their family have.

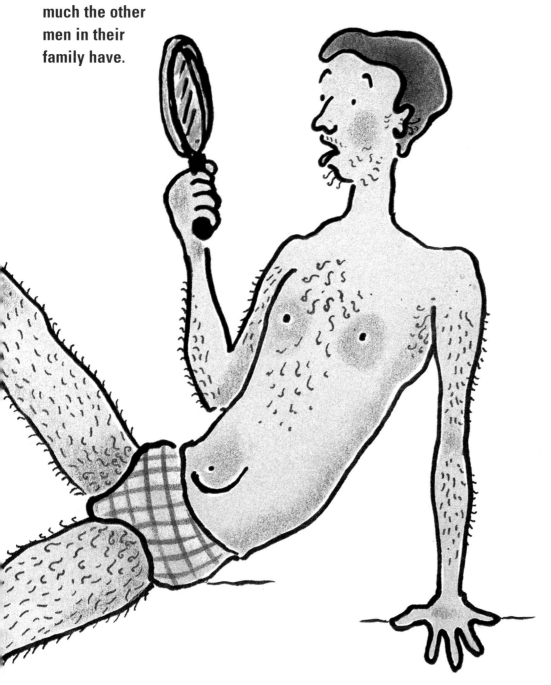

Some people are happy to leave body hair alone. Their religion may tell them not to cut their hair. Other people may want to remove body hair. For example, swimmers and athletes prefer to remove hair because it helps them perform better at their sports. There are different methods of removing hair to suit different parts of the body.

▲ *When speed is important, shaving can help athletes stay streamlined.*

> Todd: 'I've got some hair growing on my face but it's not long enough to shave off yet. I wish it would hurry up – it's sort of in-between.'

Being a smoothie

Boys can start shaving using a throwaway razor and soap or shaving foam. It is better to wait until you are shaving every day and your facial hair is stronger before trying an electric razor.

23

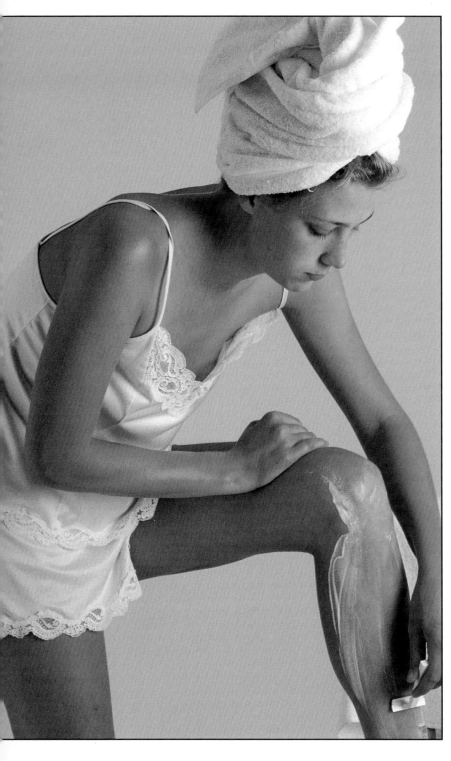

Shaving is quick and easy, but hair starts to grow back immediately and is thicker and more stubbly. Some girls may decide to shave the hair on their legs and under their arms.

Girls should not shave their faces, thighs or around the bikini line because the hair can grow back stubbly and itchy. Try using a special cream that dissolves the hair so it can be washed away, or try waxing using wax strips or a hot wax kit. Both these methods last longer than shaving.

Girls with dark hair may notice some hair growing on their faces, above the lips and on the cheeks. Facial hair can be lightened using a special cream. Ask your chemist or doctor for advice.

▲ *Shaving is one of the quickest ways of removing leg hair.*

How do I know when to start shaving?

You don't have to wait until the hair is thick before you start shaving. You could try shaving once or twice a week, until you need to shave every day.

> 66 Anne: 'I felt a bit embarrassed about the hair round my bikini line, so I've started to use a special cream to remove it, especially in the summer.' 99

INSIDE BOYS

Important changes that you can't see are happening inside your body. At puberty, hormones tell your sex organs to get active. A boy's testicles start making millions of sperm every day.

Sperm are the male cells that can join with a girl's egg cell to make a baby. Sperm are carried in semen which spurts out of a boy's penis when he gets sexually excited.

▼ *Growing up has its funny side*
   when you are with mates.

A boy's penis is soft and hangs down most of the time. When he has sex, or if he masturbates, more blood flows into the penis. This makes it become stiff and hard and it stands away from the body. This is called having an erection. When the boy reaches a climax, semen spurts out of his penis. This is called ejaculation.

During puberty, erections sometimes happen because of sexy thoughts or even because of the jogging movement of a bus or train. Try to concentrate on something else and the erection will soon go down.

Erections can happen at any age but may happen more often when a boy reaches puberty.

66 Allan: 'I once had an erection when I was coming home on the bus. It was really embarrassing. ' 99

27

Wet dreams

Boys sometimes have wet dreams. The penis gets hard and semen spurts out during the night, sometimes during sexy dreams. You may notice a damp patch on your pyjamas or sheet. Wet dreams are normal and happen often during puberty.

What's the difference between sperm and semen?

Sperm are male sex cells. Semen is the milky fluid that carries the sperm. A teaspoonful of the semen that spurts out when a boy ejaculates can contain up to 300 million sperm. Only one is needed to make a baby.

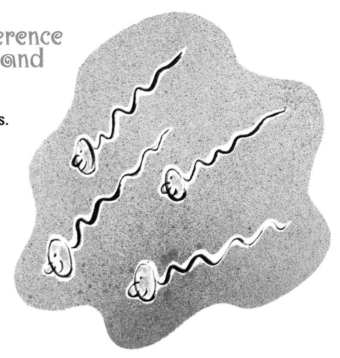

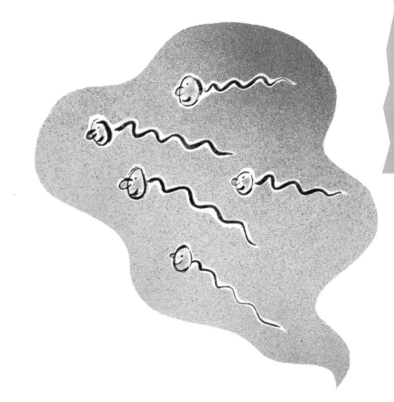

29

INSIDE GIRLS

A girl has two ovaries inside her body. They are each the size of a thumbnail but they contain thousands of tiny eggs. During puberty, hormones tell the girl's ovaries to start releasing eggs.

About once a month, an egg travels from one of the ovaries towards the girl's uterus. This is called ovulation. The uterus is shaped like an upside-down pear. It is where a baby grows during pregnancy. The uterus gets ready for a baby by making a soft lining.

If the egg doesn't join with a boy's sperm cell, the uterus lining breaks up, and the girl's body gets rid of the egg and the lining. It comes out of her body through her vagina as a dribble of blood that lasts a few days. This is called having a period or menstruating.

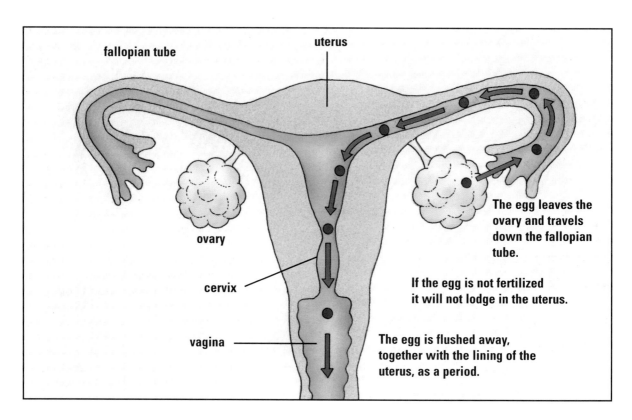

fallopian tube

uterus

ovary

cervix

vagina

The egg leaves the ovary and travels down the fallopian tube.

If the egg is not fertilized it will not lodge in the uterus.

The egg is flushed away, together with the lining of the uterus, as a period.

▲ *This diagram shows what happens inside a girl's body during her period.*

Donna: 'I always keep a note in my diary of when I start my period. It helps me to work out when the next one will begin.'

Around the time a girl's period ends, her body starts getting ready for the next egg to be released.

A girl's ovaries take turns to release eggs until she is about fifty years old, when she reaches the menopause and doesn't have periods any more. This means she can no longer become pregnant.

In between periods, girls may notice slight white or yellow staining in their pants. This is nothing to worry about – it's the vagina staying moist and cleaning itself.

When do periods start?

A girl can start having periods at any age from about nine to seventeen. Most girls have their first period when they are about twelve to fourteen years old.

Periods

It can take a year or two for a girl's periods to settle into a cycle of occurring every 2l–35 days. Many things can change the length of the cycle, such as doing exams, going on holiday or being ill.

When your period starts, you may have dragging pains (period pains) or backache. Having a warm bath, doing some gentle exercise or resting with a hot water bottle can all help. If the pains are very bad, you should see your doctor.

Sometimes, girls find they feel moody, tired and tearful just before their period. Another sign is breasts feeling tender. This is called 'PMS' (premenstrual syndrome) and is caused by changes in the levels of hormones around the time that the period is due.

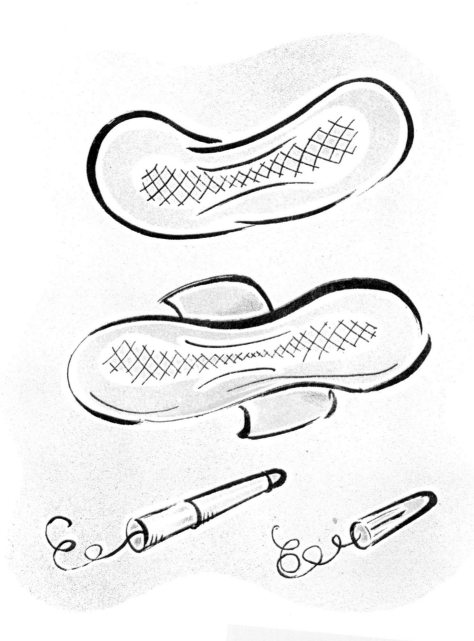

Girls can use tampons or sanitary towels during their periods. Tampons are worn inside the body. A tampon can be gently pushed into the vagina although this might take a bit of practice. Sanitary towels or pads come in a range of shapes and sizes. They usually have stick-on strips so they stay in place inside your pants.

It is very important to stay clean and fresh during your period. Tampons and towels need to be changed every two to four hours.

What if my period starts when I'm not expecting it?

Blood flow from a period is very slow – only half a cupful or so over a few days. It may help to keep a diary to work out when to expect your periods. You can also carry a spare sanitary towel or tampon with you, or wear panty liners just before your period is due.

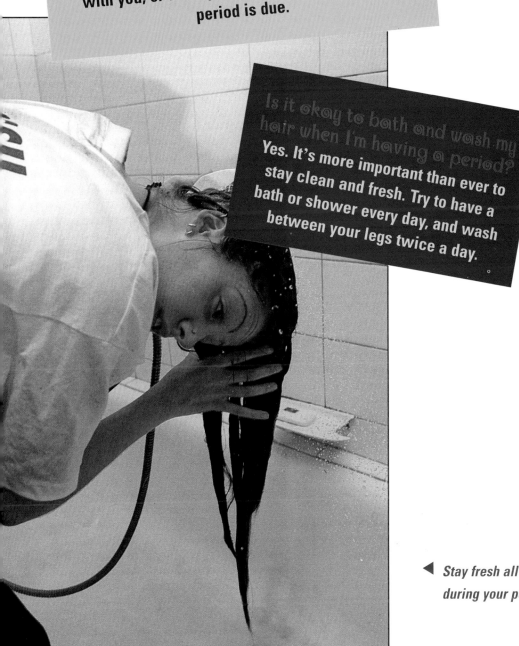

Is it okay to bath and wash my hair when I'm having a period?

Yes. It's more important than ever to stay clean and fresh. Try to have a bath or shower every day, and wash between your legs twice a day.

◀ *Stay fresh all over, especially during your period.*

35

PREGNANCY

When a girl starts having periods and a boy starts making sperm, their bodies are able to make a baby. This doesn't mean they are ready to have sex, or to be a parent.

Two cells are needed to make a baby – a female egg cell and a male sperm cell. During sex, a man's penis becomes hard and enters the woman's vagina. The penis ejaculates millions of sperm that spurt into the vagina. If the couple are not using contraception, then there is a real risk that the woman can become pregnant. It only takes one sperm to join with the female egg cell to make a baby start to grow.

The fertilized egg plants itself in the lining of the uterus and begins to divide into the different cells that make up a baby's body.

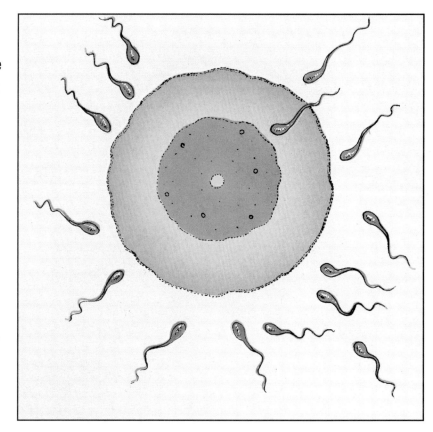

This diagram shows how sperm crowd around the egg to try to break through and fertilize it.

The uterus stretches as the baby grows, and other changes happen to the mother's body. She starts to put on weight as her belly grows larger, and her breasts grow bigger as the glands inside begin to make milk ready for the baby. Pregnancy normally lasts about forty weeks.

TRUE OR FALSE?

Can pregnancy happen

- before a girl has her first period?

- the first time a couple have sex?

- if a girl is having a period?

- if a couple have sex standing up?

- if the boy withdraws his penis before climax?

- if semen gets near the vagina, even if the penis doesn't enter it?

- if the girl washes out her vagina after sex?

YES! PREGNANCY CAN HAPPEN IN ALL THESE CASES.

Being a parent is a big responsibility. ▶

SKIN AND HAIR

During puberty, hormones can make your skin and hair start to look different. Sex hormones make the glands in your skin work harder. They pump out more sebum, the oil that keeps your skin and hair waterproof and stretchy. If sebum builds up, spots can break out on your skin. Oil glands are mostly on your face, neck and back.

Guide to healthy skin

Deal with spots by drinking plenty of water and eating lots of healthy foods like fresh fruit. Squeezing spots just makes them worse.

If the spots are red, lumpy and sore, you may need to use a special wash or cream. A doctor may give you antibiotics for acne spots, which can scar the skin.

Nat: 'I get really fed up with the spots on my face. My skin never feels really clean.'

The same glands that work in your skin can also make your hair look greasier. It helps to wash it every two to three days using a gentle shampoo.

The sweat glands in your skin are working harder too. There are a lot of sweat glands under your arms, between your legs and around your nipples. They make sweat that can start to smell if you don't wash it away regularly.

When you reach puberty, you need to wash twice a day and always after sports to stay fresh and clean. It also helps to use deodorants and antiperspirants.

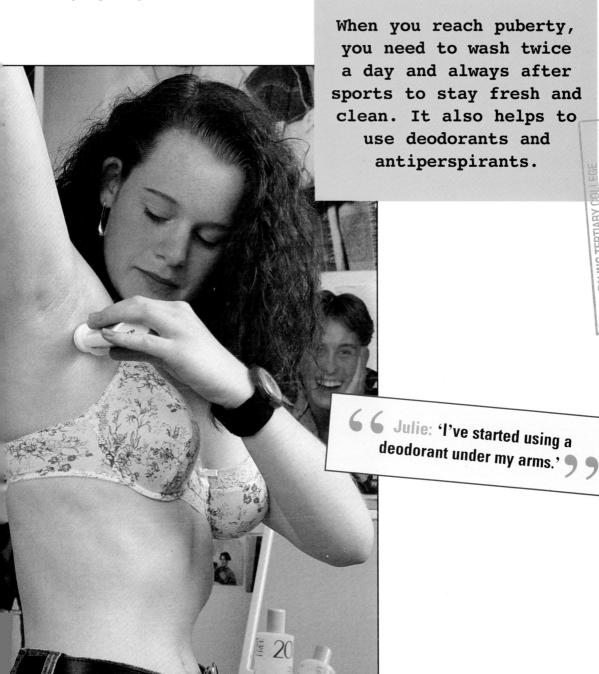

66 Julie: 'I've started using a deodorant under my arms.' 99

Getting to grips

BODY IMAGE

Am I behind?

It's normal to feel worried or uncertain when you are going through so many changes. You may worry that others the same age are ahead of you. Remember that everyone has their own bodyclock and yours is right for you.

Am I the right weight?

As your height and shape change, you may start to worry that you are looking too fat or too thin. You may spend more time looking in the mirror.

Many things shape the way we look at ourselves — pictures in magazines, models and pop stars, things people say to us.

Your image can seem ▶
extra important when
you are growing up.

Eating disorders

Magazines and other people's comments can sometimes make people think they are too fat. It's a bit like looking in one of the weird mirrors at a fair. You may start seeing yourself as too fat when really you are thin and underweight.

This can sometimes lead to eating problems such as anorexia nervosa and bulimia.

If a girl or boy has anorexia, they start dieting because they see themselves as fat even when they are dangerously thin.

People with bulimia binge on fatty, sugary foods like cakes and ice-cream, then make themselves sick so they won't put on weight.

These problems are very serious. People who have anorexia or bulimia need to see a doctor and get special help.

Your body needs to have a healthy, balance of food to be able to grow during puberty. If you are worried about your weight, go and talk to your doctor.

Worrying about your weight ▶
can lead to health problems.

GIVING YOURSELF SPACE

Remember that the changes you are going through will alter your moods too. The hormones rushing round your body can make you feel snappy and easily upset, so you row with your parents and friends. You may find yourself feeling low and wanting to cry for no reason.

Give yourself some time and space. You may want to spend more time alone, listening to your favourite music or reading a book or magazine. It can help to keep a diary to work out what's going on in your head.

Tom: 'When are you grown up? When you're allowed to drive? When you're eighteen? I think it's more to do with how you feel inside.'

Donna: 'It's been quite rough at home. Talking to my friends helps, because I know they are going through the same stuff.'

Puberty can be a difficult time. It can also be exciting and challenging.

There are some things you can't change, like how fast you grow or how tall you are. Try not to spend too much time comparing yourself to others. Try to make the best of yourself and feel good about yourself.

NOTES FOR PARENTS AND TEACHERS

The bodyclock

This chapter introduces the physical and emotional changes that take place during puberty. Students should be encouraged to discuss what is happening to their bodies (some will be obvious, such as growth spurts, others not so obvious, such as heightened emotions). They may need reassurance that these changes are normal and that their bodies will change when they are ready. Students will also need opportunities to talk to adults and with each other about their heightened emotional responses to a variety of situations.

Growing up

This chapter discusses the physical changes that take place throughout puberty; what influences adult body shape and size; diet; exercise; and rest. Students could look at family photographs to try to assess how they may look as adults. Information about balanced diets and recommended amounts of exercise and rest should be given to students. Students should be encouraged to consider how much control they can have over the choices they make, and who or what influences them when making their decisions. They should be encouraged to develop independence when making choices, to learn from unwise decisions and respect other students' differing choices.

What else is new?

The main issues here are the specific changes that take place during puberty. Students should be made aware of what will happen to those of the opposite gender and be encouraged to talk with them about those changes. They should also be given opportunities to discuss body changes with their own gender. All the information on masturbation in the chapter 'Inside boys' is equally relevant for girls.

Body hair

This chapter looks at the various types of body hair that grow during puberty. Discussions that consider why people might want to remove some of their body hair are important. It is also important that they fully understand any chosen method of hair removal. They need to be made aware that almost all methods can be painful and that some, particularly bleaching and hot wax treatments, can cause skin damage if instructions are not followed carefully. A study of the advantages and disadvantages of the various methods of hair removal would be beneficial for both boys and girls.

Inside boys

This chapter addresses the changes in the male reproductive system during puberty. It is important to emphasize that erections, ejaculations and wet dreams happen to all boys but not as frequently to some, and that masturbation is normal, and healthy and feels good but that there are private times and places that are appropriate for masturbation. Discussions about when and where masturbation is appropriate or inappropriate for both boys and girls; what might cause erections; emotional responses to erections and strategies for managing them would help students.

Inside girls

The main issue is changes that take place in the female reproductive system during puberty. It is important that information about the size and shape of human eggs is given to students so that they understand that human eggs are different from hen's eggs. Information should be given about the difference between healthy discharge and that which might indicate infections and where or who to go to for advice if they are concerned. It is important for girls to be able to discuss aspects of managing menstruation in all-girl groups. It is equally important that boys as well as girls learn about menstruation.

Making babies

This chapter covers sexual intercourse, conception, some of the changes that occur in a woman's body when she is pregnant and myths about pregnancy. Emphasis should be placed on the idea that physical readiness does not mean emotional readiness to become a parent or to start being sexually active. Information should be given about contraception and the range of contraceptive methods available. Discussions as to availability and appropriateness of the various methods are important. It is also important to discover and dispel any other myths the students may believe about having periods, getting pregnant and pregnancy.

Skin and hair

The main issues in this chapter are the increased production of sebum during puberty and how to manage personal hygiene routines. Discussions about when it might be wise to seek professional medical advice (sooner rather than later in cases of teenage acne), what types of soap and shampoo are best suited to teenage skins, which brands of deodorant are most effective and whether or not any of the brands of spot treatment work would all be relevant.

Body image

The main issues covered are weight and eating disorders, but the chapter does reinforce the bodyclock message given in chapter one. Students should discuss fantasy and reality related to body image and links to current fashion and personalities. Emphasis should be placed on the fact that however they look is OK and that there are limits to how much they can change their body shape. Students should be encouraged to be positive about their own and each other's body shape but should look at ways of altering their body shape that are realistic, sensible and do not jeopardize health. Information about who they can talk to if they have worries about their own or their friends' body image, diet or eating problems should be easily available.

Giving yourself space

This chapter briefly mentions mood swings and other emotional changes that are stronger during puberty. For many students these are more difficult to understand and manage than the physical changes. They need many opportunities to discuss who and what affects their moods and whether there are times when they are especially moody. They need to develop personal strategies for managing mood swings. Discussions should also take place that enable students to talk about their responses to each other and how their own behaviour might affect other members of the group. Parents and teachers should also discuss with students their behaviour and together look at making realistic changes.

GLOSSARY

Acne
A skin problem that usually affects teenagers. It produces sore and lumpy spots on the face, neck and back.

Antibiotics
Medicines that can kill bacteria.

Bikini line
The area where pubic hair is removed so that it does not show at either side of pants or swimsuits.

Binge
To eat uncontrollably.

Cervix
The neck of the uterus.

Climax
Highest, most intense point.

Contraception
Different methods, such as condoms and the Pill, used to stop a girl getting pregnant.

Diet
The food and drink we eat.

Egg cell
The female sex cell.

Fallopian tubes
The tubes in the body that allow egg cells to travel from the ovaries to the uterus.

Fertilized
When a male cell has joined with a female cell.

Glands
Organs in the body that make fluids such as oil, milk and sweat.

Growth spurt
The time when you grow fast.

Hormones
Chemicals made by the body.

Masturbate
To rub or stroke the clitoris or penis.

Menstruating
The monthly release of blood and the uterus lining. It begins in girls during puberty and continues into adulthood. Also called periods.

Organs
Parts of the body that have special jobs to do.

Ova
Female egg cells.

Ovaries
The female organs that produce eggs.

Panty liners
A thin towel that keeps pants fresh and clean if changed regularly.

Penis
Male sex organ.

Protein
The part of food that helps build and repair the body.

Pubic hair
Hair that grows around the sex parts.

Semen
The milky fluid that carries sperm.

Sperm
Male sex cells.

Testicles
The male organs that make sperm.

Uterus
The organ inside the female body where a baby grows during pregnancy.

Vagina
Female sex parts between a girl's legs

FURTHER INFORMATION

Books to Read

Body Sense: Your Guide to Growing Up by Karen Bryant-Mole (Health Education Authority, 1996)
Let's Discuss: Anorexia and Bulimia by Pete Sanders and Steve Myers (Watts, 1995)
Let's Discuss: Puberty and Growing Up by Pete Sanders and Steve Myers (Watts, 1995)

Leaflets to Read

How Your Body Changes by the Family Planning Association
Periods: What You Need to Know by the Family Planning Association
4 Boys: A Below the Belt Guide to the Male Body by the Family Planning Association
Boys: Looking Ahead; Girls: Looking Ahead available from Brook Advisory Centres

Videos

Growing Up and Sex Education (BBC Education, 1996)
Growing Up – A Guide to Puberty (Bounty Vision, available from the Family Planning Association)
Living and Growing (Grampian Television)

Useful organizations

Family Planning Information Service
27–35 Mortimer Street, London W1N 7RJ
Tel: 0171 636 7866

Brook Advisory Centres
165 Gray's Inn Road, London WC1X 8UD.
There should be a local Brook Advisory Centre in your area.

National Centre for Eating Disorders
54 New Road, Esher, Surrey KT10 9NU
Tel: 01372 469493

Family Planning Association
212 Pentonville Road
London N19FP

INDEX